Mit Wörterbuch und Vokabelhilfe

Martin Klein

Englisch lernen mit den Leselöwen

Torjägergeschichten

Aus dem Deutschen übersetzt von David Ingram

Zeichnungen von Heribert Schulmeyer

Loewe

Bibliografische Information Der Deutschen Bibliothek
Die Deutsche Bibliothek verzeichnet diese Publikation in der Deutschen Nationalbibliografie; detaillierte bibliografische Daten sind im Internet über *http://dnb.ddb.de* abrufbar.

Der Umwelt zuliebe ist dieses Buch auf chlorfrei gebleichtem Papier gedruckt.

ISBN 3-7855-5334-X – 1. Auflage 2005

Die deutsche Originalausgabe erschien 1999 im Loewe Verlag unter dem Titel „Leselöwen-Torjägergeschichten"
Aus dem Deutschen übersetzt von David Ingram
Umschlagillustration: Heribert Schulmeyer
Umschlaggestaltung: Andreas Henze

www.loewe-verlag.de

Contents

Liebe Eltern,

unaufhaltsam hält die englische Sprache Einzug in den kindlichen Wortschatz. Was die Sprachwissenschaft nüchtern als Anglizismen betitelt, finden die Kinder überaus spannend. Mit ungebremstem Wissensdurst machen sie sich daran, erste Worte oder Sätze in einer Fremdsprache zu erlernen und zu kommunizieren.

Kinder sind relativ früh mit dem Englischen vertraut, spätestens seit der Einführung des Englischunterrichts an den Grundschulen. Eine Fremdsprache spielerisch, ohne Erfolgszwang, dafür aber mit schnellen Erfolgserlebnissen lernen, so lautet das Motto.
Dieses Prinzip haben wir auch den Englisch-Ausgaben unserer Erstlese-Reihe *Leselöwen* zu Grunde gelegt. In abgeschlossenen Geschichten können die kindlichen Leser ihre ersten Englischkenntnisse anwenden und vertiefen. Die Sprache ist einfach gehalten, die wichtigsten Vokabeln sind im Text markiert und werden in ihrer konkreten Bedeutung am Rand auf Deutsch erklärt. Verben werden dabei gleich in der jeweiligen Person, Adjektive in der flektierten

Form übersetzt. Der Sinn eines Satzes lässt sich so schnell und ohne lästiges Nachschlagen erschließen. Viele Begriffe werden zusätzlich in den Illustrationen durch Wort-Bildzuweisungen erläutert.
Im Anhang finden sich sowohl die wichtigsten Vokabeln aus dem Text in alphabetischer Reihenfolge als auch ein speziell dem jeweiligen Thema zu Grunde gelegter Wortschatz auf einer praktischen Ausklappseite.
Die Verben stehen hier im Infinitiv, da an dieser Stelle der Hauptakzent eher auf der Erweiterung des Wortschatzes als auf der Erschließung eines Wortes innerhalb eines Satzes liegt. Dabei werden nicht alle möglichen Bedeutungen im Deutschen angegeben, sondern nur die wichtigsten.
Und wenn Sie mit Ihrem Kind gleichzeitig auch das Hörverständnis und die Sprechfertigkeit trainieren möchten, sind bei Jumbo zu jedem englischen *Leselöwen*-Band die entsprechenden Hörkassetten erhältlich.

Viel Spaß und Erfolg mit
„Englisch lernen mit den Leselöwen“
wünscht Ihnen Ihr

Leselöwen-Englisch-Team

MSC

Beaten by Glückstadt

Unbelievable! Impossible! Astonishing! But it's true. Holger sits on the grandstand. He watches the first team playing football. He shakes his head in amazement. He feels as if he is under a very cold shower.

Holger is so astonished because of three letters. MSC. His football club. He plays for their junior team. He knows all the players in the first team. Their trainer Uli, for instance, and his uncle Jörg who plays as a winger.

The three letters MSC are an important part of Holger's life. Holger looks at his piece of paper again. It shows the course of the tournament.

Unglaublich; Unmöglich

Verwunderlich

Verblüffung

als ob

überrascht

zum Beispiel

Außen-/Flügelstürmer

Turnier

This is because Holger likes to write down the results of football matches in advance:

Ergebnisse
im Voraus

Quarter-final:
MSC-Fortuna-Glückstadt
5:0 (or higher)

Semi-final:
MSC-Turnsport Süden 3:0 (or 3:1 or maybe 4:2 at worst but a win anyway with at least 2 goals difference)

Final:
MSC-Borussia Friedrichsfelde
2:0 (perhaps one goal against us, but otherwise well-deserved)

Viertelfinale
trotzdem; mindestens
Toren Unterschied
vielleicht
ansonsten; wohlverdient

Holger crumples up the sheet of paper in a ball, stands up, and angrily stomps over to the waste-paper bin by the stairs. Then he throws the ball into the bin and kicks it really hard.

knüllt zusammen
stapft
Abfalleimer

The bin makes a loud clang. Holger cannot believe that his team can lose.

A big score board above the pitch shows the score of the game between MSC and Fortuna Glückstadt, a really pathetic team in a lower league. The players are all useless, they can't play football at all, and in the first round they lost every single one of their games.

Anzeigetafel
Spielfeld; Punktestand
armseliges; niedrigeren
unbrauchbar
verloren

Holger remembers how badly Glückstadt played in the previous rounds: twice 0:0 and one 1:1. The MSC record is much better: 7:0, 4:1 and 5:2. Jens, the big centre-forward from MSC, nicknamed Balu, scored all seven of the goals in the first game. In the last game he even scored a hat-trick!

erinnert sich

Vorrunden; zweimal

Liste

Mittelstürmer

mit Spitznamen; erzielte

So the goal average for MSC is 16:3 and 6:0 points, as compared to 1:1 goals and 3:3 points for Glückstadt. Everyone expects MSC to beat Glückstadt very easily. But Jens misses two clear chances, and in midfield, Hassan Ben Brahim gives away a penalty. Winger Jörg Werda tries to kick the ball straight into the goal from

Durchschnitt

im Vergleich zu

erwartet

schlagen

verpasst

Mittelfeld

Elfmeter

direkt

a sharp angle instead of passing it to Balu. Trainer Uli, uncle Jörg and right winger Stefan Porwall only hit the post and the crossbar.

spitzem (schlechtem) Winkel; statt

Pfosten; (Tor-)Latte

Two minutes before the end, a Glückstadt player scores a goal. This is the first time that one of the players is near the MSC goal.

Then the final whistle: 0:1. MSC, the favourites, are out of the tournament. It's all over.

Schlusspfiff

Holger cannot believe the bitter truth. He kicks the metal refuse container again, even harder this time.

Wahrheit

metallenen Müllbehälter

CLANG! He wants to kick it as far as the Milky Way, that stupid dustbin with all his stupid predictions inside it!

Milchstraße

Mülltonne

Voraussagen; darin

"Hey, what do you think you're doing?" an old man asks.

"All right, we lost, but that's no reason to break things!"

Holger walks away. That old man doesn't understand how he feels: how angry he is, and how disappointed.

Suddenly Holger feels a sweaty hand on his shoulder.

Uli stands behind him on the stairs that lead up the grandstand. He looks tired and exhausted. Holger can see the deep disappointment in his eyes.

reason – Grund; *break* – kaputtzumachen
how – wie
disappointed – enttäuscht
Suddenly – Plötzlich
sweaty – verschwitzte
shoulder – Schulter
tired – müde
exhausted – erschöpft
deep – tiefe
disappointment – Enttäuschung

Uli says to Holger: "Have you ever experienced anything like this? I haven't." Some people see the MSC player on the grandstand, and soon there is a small crowd around him.

"Bad luck, really bad luck!" one man says.

"What a terrible game!" another says.

"If you can't score a goal against those idiots, then it's your own fault."

"What an embarrassing match!"

"It was awful!"

Uli not only looks exhausted, he also looks very unhappy.

"Why does everybody bother poor Uli?" Holger thinks. He turns to the crowd of people and says loudly:

Hast du jemals … erlebt

Menschenmenge

Pech

schreckliches

eigene Schuld

peinliches

furchtbar

erschöpft

quält

armen

"Can you please tell me how one team can beat another team if it has a run of bad luck?!"

The astonished people in the crowd say nothing.

"You see? It's impossible, isn't it?" Holger says.

His trainer grins: "You're right, actually."

He gives Holger a friendly pat on the shoulder. "Next time they'll be the ones with the bad luck. We'll beat them at least ten – nil."

Holger nods. He knows the trainer is right.

schlagen; ein anderes

eine Pechsträhne

erstaunten

unmöglich

oder?

grinst

wirklich

Klaps

mindestens mit 10:0

nickt

Pelé, Gerd Müller, Tillmann Schmitz

Tillmann stands in the middle of the football pitch. He looks nervous. He waits for the referee to blow his whistle for the start of the game. His fellow player Jens waits for the whistle, too.

Spielfeld

Schiedsrichter; blasen

Mannschafts-kamerad

The moment the referee blows it, Jens and Tillmann will rush into the other team's penalty area. That is their plan.

Today, in the game against Eintracht Husen, Tillmann wants to play like Pelé, the three-time world soccer champion from Brazil, and Gerd Müller, the best German goal-scorer of all time.

Does Tillmann have anything in common with them at all? Apart from the fact that he plays the same sport?

Pelé's club is the legendary FC Santos from Sao Paolo in Brazil. Gerd Müller's club is the glorious Bayern München from Germany. Tillmann plays on the junior team of Borussia Wickede.

werden stürmen

Strafraum

wie

Fußball-weltmeister

gemeinsam

Abgesehen von der Tatsache

ruhmreiche

So it's not the club.

Pelé is the most famous football player in the world. Everyone knows Gerd Müller, too. But Tillmann is completely unknown.

So it's not the fame either.

Pelé usually wore the number 10 shirt. Gerd Müller preferred the number 13 shirt, especially during national games. Tillmann prefers to wear the number 7.

most famous – *berühmteste*
completely – *völlig*
unknown – *unbekannt*
not the fame either – *auch nicht der Ruhm*
wore – *trug*
preferred – *bevorzugte*
especially – *vor allem*

It's not a typical shirt, but Tillmann played his first game in it.

So it's not the number either.

So what else do they all have in common? Maybe they like fish and chips? Maybe they all like terriers? Perhaps they like to read adventure stories?

No, they don't have any of those things in common either.

auch nicht die Nummer

was sonst

gemeinsam

Abenteuer

"I know what you do have in common," says Mr. Schmitz, Tillmann's father. "You're all excellent goal-scorers!"

Really great footballers.

Players who can outwit all their opponents.	überlisten / Gegner
Players who are always in the right place at the right time, and always score excellent goals.	schießen
Players who everybody fears, and watches very closely.	fürchtet / genau
Perfect attackers.	Tadellose Angreifer
Kings of the penalty area.	Strafraum
Brilliant dribblers.	
Genuine artists.	Echte Künstler

Players who score more goals in a year than others do in their entire careers.

Tillmann knows exactly how many goals he has scored. Almost three years ago he gave his father a results book.

The first entry says:

schießen
ganzen Karriere
wie
geschossen hat
Ergebnisheft
Eintrag; lautet

Home game:
Against: TURA Asseln
Result: 3:3 (1:2) (the result in brackets is the score at half-time.)
Goals by Tillmann: 2 (one with the left foot for the 1:0, one with the right in a solo to make the final result 3:3)

Klammern

Today is Tillmann's 62nd game, and in the 61st so far he has scored 67 goals! More than a goal per game on average! Hardly anyone can beat that!

im Durchschnitt pro Spiel
Kaum

"Only two people, actually," Tillmann's father says proudly. "Pelé and Gerd Müller!"

Gerd Müller, centre-forward for the German team in the 1970 and 1974 World Cup championships, scored a total of 68 times in his 62 national games! Gerd Müller was brilliant.

tatsächlich

stolz

Mittelstürmer

schoss

Mr. Schmitz knows only one other player who scored more goals than Gerd Müller: Pelé. The Brazilian scored 77 times! — *schoss*

"But he needed 92 games to do that, Tillmann," Mr. Schmitz said. "I bet you'll do better than him." — *wette; du wirst machen*

"Pelé can wait", Tillmann thinks. First he has to beat Gerd Müller's record. — *schlagen*

Tillmann gets ready to play. He knows this is a very important day. He waits for the referee to blow his whistle. — *Schiedsrichter; blasen*

Tillmann just needs one goal, one single goal. Then he will be as successful in the junior team of Borussia Wickede as Gerd Müller was in the German national team. — *einziges; wird sein; erfolgreich*

The referee blows his whistle, and the game begins!

Tillmann runs forward immediately, and Jens stays behind slightly.

That's the way they always do it. It's their special style.

But the game doesn't go the way Tillmann expects.

Their opponents, Eintracht Husen, are powerful, and keep them under a lot of pressure.

Tillmann hardly ever gets the ball. His team only gets close to the enemy penalty area on one occasion. Tillmann suddenly runs free, but Jens tries to score himself instead of passing the ball to Tillmann. The goalkeeper catches the ball.

"Why didn't you pass it to me?" Tillmann complains.

sofort
ein wenig
sich vorstellt
Gegner
stark
Druck
nah
gegnerischen Strafraum
Gelegenheit
plötzlich
schießen
statt
Torwart
beschwert sich

Now it's the second half, and the score is still 0:0. Tillmann gets two good chances, but misses both of them.

verfehlt

He gets his next chance just one minute before the end of the game. It's still 0:0. He traps a long ball in the middle of the enemy penalty area. Then he gets ready to kick the ball at the goal with his right foot. "Now," he thinks to himself. "Now's my chance."

stoppt

gegnerischen Strafraum

But the angle to the goal is too narrow.

There's hardly enough room to take a shot at goal.

"I think I can do it," Tillmann says.

Suddenly, at the last moment, the captain from the other team arrives and forces Tillmann away from the goal.

Winkel
eng
Plötzlich
zwingt

Now the angle is even narrower.

Jens is in front of the goal.

"Cross it!" he shouts. "Cross it!"

Tillmann gets ready to kick the ball.

What will he do? Pelé would have done an elegant cross. Gerd Müller would have scored a seemingly impossible goal.

But Tillmann is neither Pelé nor Gerd Müller.

Winkel

enger

wird er tun

hätte elegant quer gespielt

hätte geschossen

allem Anschein nach

weder … noch

GOAL!

Salomon scores two

Football sometimes is complicated. A lot of decisions have to be made during a game.

kompliziert; Entscheidungen

müssen getroffen werden

Which side gets the throw-in? Did the defender foul the other player, or did he play the ball? Did the foul happen in the penalty area or just outside it?

Mannschaft; Einwurf; Verteidiger; foulen

Strafraum

People ask questions like these at football matches all over the world.

The best person to answer them is someone who does not take sides.

Salomon Neutrum, the hero of this story, is that kind of important person.

Salomon Neutrum is a referee.

wichtige

Schiedsrichter

He wears black clothes, and tries as hard as he can to do his job. A referee's job is often difficult, and sometimes he can make mistakes, just like a player. Referees know that nobody is perfect.

gibt sich große Mühe

Schiedsrichter

Lots of fans and footballers don't agree, and they get angry with a referee for the smallest mistake. The worst ones are the people who get angry with the referee even when he is right.

sind nicht einverstanden

And those are the kind of people in Salomon's football match today. The game is between Eintracht Neudorf and Spielvereinigung Altstadt. The two teams are full of players who do nothing but complain to the referee the whole time!

Art

sich beschweren

ganze

The benches beside the football pitch are empty. That is not surprising. Nobody wants to watch football teams that complain all the time. The only people at the edge of the pitch are the two trainers, and a handful of substitutes.

surprising: überraschend
complain: sich beschweren
at the edge of: am Rande
pitch: Spielfeld
substitutes: Ersatzspieler

Salomon knows the two teams very well. He knows that whenever he blows his whistle, they criticize him. Even if there is an offside, or handball, they never agree with Salomon.

whenever: wann auch immer; blows: bläst
criticize: kritisieren
offside: Abseits

There is only one thing that both teams agree on: “It’s the referee’s fault!”

And that makes Salomon very angry.

He blows his whistle to start the game.

Ten minutes later, Altstadt gets their first corner.

“Hey, ref, I didn’t touch the ball!” a defender from Neudorf shouts.

Next, one of the Altstadt players fouls his opponent. Salomon awards a free kick to Neudorf.

“Hey ref, I never touched him!” the Altstadt player shouts.

The referee shows him the yellow card.

“He must be blind!” the trainer from Altstadt says.

Schiedsrichters Schuld

bläst

Ecke

Gegenspieler

spricht zu

A little later an Altstadt player traps the ball on the line. Is the ball out of play, or not? Salomon blows his whistle: a free kick for Neudorf.

"Whaaat?" the Altstadt player says. "The ball was in!!"

bläst

"If you carry on like this, you're going to get a nasty surprise," Salomon thinks to himself.

weitermachst
wirst du bekommen; scheußliche
Überraschung

And things do carry on in the same way. The Altstadt players make lots of mistakes, and so do the players from Neudorf. And each time they make them, they always blame the referee.

die Schuld geben; Schiedsrichter

At half time, the score is nil all.

Punktestand; Null

"Buy yourself a pair of glasses, ref!" an Altstadt player shouts.

"You're useless!" a Neudorf player says, and looks angrily at Salomon.

unbrauchbar

"Just wait," Salomon thinks to himself. "I've had enough of you lot. You're in for a big surprise."

Jetzt habe ich aber genug!

In the 65th minute, there is a corner for Neudorf. Salomon stands in just the right position in front of the goal, and when the ball comes over he heads it in!

1:0!

The Altstadt players are stunned.

Ecke

fassungslos

"Sorry," Salomon says. "I was in the wrong place at the wrong time."

"The goal doesn't count, does it?!" an Altstadt player stammers.

"Of course it does," Salomon answers. "If a ball bounces off a referee into the net, it's still a goal."

"We're going to protest about that!" the Altstadt trainer shouts.

zählt

stottert

zurückprallt von

Schiedsrichter

His players are furious, but they continue with the game. They don't want to lose. *wütend* *setzen fort*

Salomon decides to help the Altstadt players. Just before the end of the game, the ball lands in front of his feet.

He gives it a big kick. The Neudorf goalkeeper has no chance. *Torwart*

1:1.

The final result is justified. *gerechtfertigt*

Beach football in Brazil

Erich sits on the beach and buries his bare feet in the warm sand. He watches two football teams playing on the beach. The players are barefooted, and the goals are small. They look a bit like the ones in ice hockey. There are no lines on the sand. The sea is on one side, and sunbathing tourists are on the other. Sometimes the ball lands in the water, and sometimes it lands on the belly of a tourist.

vergräbt; nackten

barfuß

ein Sonnenbad nehmende

Bauch

Erich looks out across the Atlantic Ocean. "Africa must be over there, somewhere beyond the horizon," he thinks to himself.

hinter dem Horizont

barefooted

Europe is over there, with Germany right in the middle of it. Thousands of kilometres away. But it only takes ten hours to get there. Erich starts to feel a bit homesick.

Back at home he always plays football with his friends. He plays during the morning break at school, with Gustav, Eckhard and Olaf and the other boys from his class. He also plays football on Tuesday afternoons in the junior team.

Erich looks over his shoulder. His parents are there, sunbathing. Beyond them, Erich can see the green of the palm trees, and behind them there are lots of tall skyscrapers. Inside one of them is the holiday apartment where he and his parents are staying.

dauert

bisschen Heimweh

und nehmen ein Sonnenbad

Palmen

Wolkenkratzer

wohnen

Wow! Two weeks in Brazil, the home of football! It sounds great. Erich sighs. The last ten days were the same as Mallorca last year: beach, hotel and restaurant, restaurant, beach and hotel.

Things are also different in Recife, of course. The menus are not in German, but luckily they still have hamburgers and chips. In Mallorca there are no children begging. Here the waiters chase them away from the tables.

seufzt
dieselben
Speisekarten
betteln
verjagen

"Poor children," Erich's mother says, and gives them a few Cruzeiros. Those are Brazilian pennies.

"Obrigado," they answer. That means "thank you".

"You can't give money to everybody," Erich's father says.

Some of the children here have wooden shoe-cleaning kits.

Holzkisten mit Schuhputzzeug

Suddenly Erich recognises one of the shoe-cleaning children – he is in the football game. He really knows how to kick the ball. His best trick is dribbling.

Plötzlich; erkennt wieder

Most of the children are really good at football. Even the tall boy with the two wooden crutches who plays in goal. He is really brilliant.

Krücken

Sometimes he uses his crutches like hockey sticks. His goal is much smaller than a normal one, of course, but he is a very skilful player.

The Brazilian children lose the ball now and then, and not everything they do is clever. Erich starts to think: "Perhaps I can join in with them after all …"

hockey sticks – Hockeyschläger
skilful – geschickter
now and then – von Zeit zu Zeit
join in – sich anschließen

But Erich's plane leaves for home in four days' time.

It is high time for Erich to ask whether he can join in with the children.

Today he is closer to them than ever before.

But Erich is shy. If only he were braver!

Suddenly a deflected shot lands not far away from him. Erich gets up, traps the ball elegantly, and then kicks it back very accurately to the shoe-cleaning boy. He gives the thumbs-up. Erich makes the same sign with his hand as well. It's a popular gesture in Brazil. The goalkeeper waves at Erich with one of his crutches.

"Quer jogar?" he asks. "Vem! Vem!"

fliegt ab

höchste Zeit

zusammenkommen

schüchtern

mutiger

Plötzlich; abgefälschter

genau

streckt den Daumen nach oben

beliebte

Geste

Torwart; winkt zu

Krücken

Erich does not understand Portuguese. But he understands exactly what the children want to say.

"Beckenbauer?" the Brazilian children ask.

"Pelé!" Erich says. "Ronaldo!"

The goalkeeper laughs and throws the ball to him. Erich joins in the game.

Torwart

schließt sich an

The penalty

The defender tries to get the ball, and fouls the centre-forward. The referee blows his whistle loudly, and points at the penalty spot. Nobody protests.

Verteidiger

Mittelstürmer

Schiedsrichter; bläst

Elfmeterpunkt

Frank places the ball very carefully on the penalty spot.

Thomas, the goalkeeper, watches him.

He spits into his gloves.

He always does that before a penalty.

If Frank gets this goal, his team will win, because the score is 2 all at the moment and there are only five minutes left.

"I must catch the ball," Thomas thinks. "I've got to."

One of the players on Thomas's team whispers: "Hey, Thomas, this man shoots his penalties to the bottom left. That means to the right from your point of view."

Elfmeterpunkt

Torwart

spuckt in; Handschuhe

Elfmeter

wird gewinnen

Punktestand

flüstert

nach links unten

von dir aus gesehen

Thomas nods. Meanwhile, Frank looks at the goalkeeper, and then looks up at the left-hand corner. He turns round and walks back a short way, thinking: "That'll make the goalkeeper nervous."

In goal, Thomas thinks: "I bet he's more nervous than I am. Nobody gets angry with a

nickt; unterdessen

Torwart

linke

Ecke

Das wird

goalkeeper if he misses a penalty. That's because he has less of a chance. All the pressure is on the man who kicks the ball."

The other players are now outside the penalty area. Now only Frank, Thomas and the referee are left inside it. Frank waits a short distance away

Torwart; verfehlt
Elfmeter
hat eine kleinere Chance
Druck
Strafraum
Schiedsrichter
Entfernung

from the ball, with his hands on his hips. Thomas waits on the line, ready to jump and catch the ball.

Hüften

Frank thinks: "The goalkeeper thinks it's a trick. He thinks I'm going to kick the ball to the right. That's why he'll jump to the right. But I'm actually going to kick to the left."

Torwart

ich werde schießen

tatsächlich

"He looked very hard at my right-hand corner," Thomas thinks. "I wonder if it's a trick. Or perhaps he isn't so clever."

frage mich

Everything is ready for the penalty kick. The referee blows his whistle.

Schiedsrichter

bläst

Frank starts his run-up.

trabt los

He decides to take five steps before he kicks the ball.

Now he only has four steps left.

"Perhaps the goalkeeper knows that I prefer to kick to the left when I take penalties," thinks Frank. "So I'd better kick to the right."

In goal, Thomas moves slightly. He hopes that it makes Frank more nervous.

Torwart

bevorzuge

Elfmeter

ich sollte besser

leicht

Just three steps left before the shot.

"He's going to kick it low to the left or low to the right," Thomas thinks. "It certainly won't be a high shot. They never dare to do that. Shooting a ball into the top corner of a goal is difficult and risky."

"Maybe I should just kick it straight into the middle for a change," Frank thinks. "After all, the goalkeeper is going to jump into the left or the right corner."

There are two steps left before the shot.

"I'll keep my eye on the ball and just wait and see," Thomas thinks. The thoughts flash through his head like lightning.

links unten

wagen

Ecke

riskant

Torwart; wird springen

Ich werde

sausen

Blitz

Frank feels just the same.
Just one step left.
He gets ready to kick.
Just before Frank kicks it, Thomas dives through the air. Towards his left.
Frank kicks the ball hard at his favourite, left-hand corner.

Kurz bevor

springt

Ecke

Thomas has no chance! He flies in the wrong direction.

But the ball doesn't land in the goal!

Frank's shot is too careful. The ball bounces off the goalpost!

Bad luck, Frank. That's football!

prallt zurück

Torpfosten

Pech

Dein Wörterbuch A–I

A	actually	tatsächlich, wirklich, eigentlich, übrigens
	adventure	Abenteuer
	another	noch eine, -r, -s, ein zweiter, ein anderer
	anyway	irgendwie, ohnehin, sowieso, trotzdem
	anywhere	irgendwo(hin), wo … auch (immer), überall (hin)
	as compared to	im Vergleich zu
	as if	als ob
	astonishing	erstaunlich; verwunderlich
	at least	wenigstens, mindestens
	awful	furchtbar, scheußlich
B	belly	Bauch
	brave	mutig, unerschrocken, tapfer
C	closely	dicht, eng, genau
	completely	völlig, ganz, vollständig
	crowd	Menschenmenge, Gedränge

D	decision	Entscheidung, Beschluss
	deep	tief
	disappointed	enttäuscht
	disappointment	Enttäuschung
	dustbin	Mülltonne
E	especially	(ganz) besonders, vor allem
F	for instance	zum Beispiel
	for short	kurz
H	hardly	kaum, fast nicht
	how	wie, wieso
I	immediately	sofort
	important	wichtig
	impossible	unmöglich
	in advance	im Voraus
	in common	gemeinsam
	instead of	stattdessen, anstelle von

Dein Wörterbuch L–T

L	like	wie
M	meanwhile	inzwischen, unterdessen
N	narrow	schmal, eng
	(not) … either	auch nicht
	now and then	ab und zu, gelegentlich
O	occasion	Gelegenheit, Möglichkeit, Anlass
	otherwise	sonst, ansonsten, im Übrigen
P	perhaps	vielleicht
	point of view	Standpunkt
	poor	arm
	powerful	mächtig, stark, einflussreich
	proudly	stolz
R	reason	Grund, Verstand, Vernunft
S	shoulder	Schulter

S	shy	schüchtern
	single	einzig, allein, einzeln, einfach
	straight	gerade, direkt
	successful	erfolgreich
	suddenly	plötzlich
	surprising	überraschend; erstaunlich
T	terrible	schrecklich, furchtbar, fürchterlich
	the same	der, die, das Gleiche; der-, die-, dasselbe
	tired	müde
	to agree	einverstanden sein, sich einigen
	to bet	wetten
	to blame	die Schuld geben; tadeln
	to break	kaputtmachen, (zer)brechen, zerreißen
	to carry on	weitermachen, fortsetzen
	to complain	klagen, sich beklagen, sich beschweren

Dein Wörterbuch T–W

T	to continue	fortsetzen, weitermachen mit
	to count	zählen, rechnen
	to dare	wagen, riskieren, sich trauen
	to expect	erwarten, annehmen, vermuten
	to fear	(be)fürchten
	to grin	grinsen
	to join	teilnehmen, sich anschließen, zusammenkommen
	to leave for	abfahren, abreisen nach
	to nod	nicken
	to prefer	vorziehen, bevorzugen, lieber haben/tun
	to recognize	(wieder) erkennen
	to remember	sich erinnern (an), denken an
	to sigh	seufzen
	to stammer	stottern
	to stomp	stapfen
	to wave at	zuwinken
	to whisper	flüstern